My Father's Oaks

My Father's Oaks

DUANE K. CAYLOR

RESOURCE *Publications* • Eugene, Oregon

MY FATHER'S OAKS

Resource Publications
An Imprint of Wipf and Stock Publishers
199 W. 8th Ave., Suite 3
Eugene, OR 97401

www.wipfandstock.com

PAPERBACK ISBN: 979-8-3852-8167-1
HARDCOVER ISBN: 979-8-3852-8168-8
EBOOK ISBN: 979-8-3852-8169-5
VERSION NUMBER 05/07/26

For my wife, Nancy, and our daughters, Heather, Heidi, and Hannah, and in memory of our son, Elijah Duane

CONTENTS

ACKNOWLEDGMENTS

Thank you to the editors of the following journals, in which most of the poems in this book, occasionally in modified form, first appeared:

Able Muse: "Cicero Comments"

Atlanta Review: "At the Church Picnic," "Stopping with Our Daughters to Watch Horses," "Sunday Morning in His Workshop," "The Ghost of Dr. C. Sargent Ferris Defends Himself"

Blue Unicorn: "Alone in November Above Lock and Dam Number 11," "Corrupted Bears," "Drive-Thru," "Grass Will Find the Smallest Crack," "Honey Wagon," "Rabbit and Coyote," "The Death of James the Just," "The Fall of Rome," "What Orpheus Remembers"

Formalist: "Snow-Blind"

First Things: "Christmas Caroling in Colonial Williamsburg," "Drought Breaker," "Francis After Collestrada," "Journey into Autumn," "Political Calendar," "Ruins," "Stealing Pears," "The Day the Rain Began," "Why I Plant Redbuds"

Hellas: "Nancy After Her Bath," "Oranges," "The Way of Geese," "Yellow-Eyed Grackle"

Kansas Quarterly: "Ever After," "Going Home"

Lamp-Post of the Southern California C. S. Lewis Society: "A Supplication," "Two Songs"

Light: "Muskellunge Creek," "Philanthropist"

Lyric: "Early Girls," "Dénouement," "For a Young Son Far from Home," "Grand Army," "Like Balaam," "Oregon Trail"

Measure: "Learning Curve at the NKVD," "Praying with Emerson"

Midwest Quarterly: "Lovers' Leap"

Nebo: "Plate Tectonics"

Off the Coast: "Daphne," "Memorandum from Wadi Kerith," "Uncle Henry and the Virgin"

Plains Poetry Journal: "Diabetes Mellitus," "Nebuchadnezzar Restored," "The Suicide Speaks"

Raintown Review: "Genetic Load," "Sixth Street Wharf"

Slant: "Anonymous Creek," "Mississippi Rhinoceros," "My Father's Oaks," "Pascal's Good Night," "Pasternak, 1956," "Walnuts"

Society of Classical Poets: "Edward Hicks: *An Indian Summer View of the Farm and Stock of James C. Cornell, 1848*," "Lenin," "Watching Television Coverage of the Fire at Notre Dame de Paris, April 15, 2019"

South Coast Poetry Journal: "What Ptolemy Knew"

Think: "The Young Widow Braids Her Daughter's Hair," "Walking the Dead End Together in Late Autumn"

Thirteen: "Loss of Light," "Moonrise"

TRINACRIA: "Apelles Paints Alexander the Great," "A New Mother in Sparta"

APELLES PAINTS ALEXANDER THE GREAT

At Ephesus (and Aristotle's goad),
Apelles painted Macedon astride
Bucephalus. Then just upon the road
of conquest, further down the road of pride,
young Alexander did not like mimesis
such as informed Apelles's artistry,
and put the painter through a catechesis
on portraiture as ideology.
Apelles, though, refused to simply pander,
and had Bucephalus brought in to view
the work. The horse, on seeing Alexander
portrayed in paint, neighed, proving painter true.
Still Alexander found the work no use
and had Apelles dress him up as Zeus.

SUNDAY MORNING IN HIS WORKSHOP

Left at the ready, a button-headed brace
rests on the bench, awaiting a command
to spin once more. With augur bit in place,
it translates languages of mind and hand
into a solid runic poetry.
Beside the drill, a wood plane seems to float
on waves of scalloped shavings out to sea,
its prow scrolled skyward like a dragon boat.
The other tools attend at ease: the awls,
screwdrivers, chisels, mallets, saws, and pliers
grouped family, genus, species on the walls
and shelves as their utility requires.
A broom and pan lean on an empty chair,
and cedar incense fills the golden air.

POLITICAL CALENDAR

Spring like a popular insurrection rises
against a winter government's assizes;

gone mad by June, its liberality
gives way to summer's fruitful anarchy.

Order returns in autumn as the air
with libertarian chill grows doctrinaire.

Displacing fall, the winter vows to keep
a Tory world, conservative in sleep.

This pattern follows year in and year out
as ideologies are put to rout

at equinox and solstice. So we neither
despair nor glory in the change of weather.

This state of things should discipline our zeal:
all policies will one day face repeal,

all present institutions cede their powers
eventually to circumstance and hours.

Upon this spinning earth, we will not find
a government to permanently bind.

For as with seasons, with affairs of men,
what goes around will come around again.

JOURNEY INTO AUTUMN

Once again we are on the road early,
driving to see our son wrestle with cancer for gold.
A cloud bank falls like a heavy eyelid
over the eastern sky, crowding
the tender light against the horizon—
healthy crimson, healthy orange compressed
by gray as thick as blasts in leukemic marrow.
Birds fly everywhere:
electrons energized to higher shells
by even this meager dawn.
Life will, life must make do on little.

What do you think of all the beauty
squandered along this mournful road?
Tragedy may induce myopia.
Still, I notice the distant trees like a remembrance of your hair,
the light on the fields the color of your neck, the
unseen sun's halo dark and pink as one of your areolae.
Turning on the radio, I hear again of
Christ as God's sufficient grace, and I think
of our young son clinging gracefully to life like
the stubborn leaves on
red November oaks.

LEARNING CURVE AT THE NKVD

"Show me the man, and I will find you the crime."
—Lavrentiy Beria

We kept him standing naked in his cell
for three weeks, stiff as Marxist argument,
and propped him up again each time he fell,
then beat him to encourage he repent
and talk. Our efforts left an Indonesia
of bruises on his face and trunk as he
became, while begging us for anesthesia,
an atlas of our fear's cartography.
He finally told us what we had suspected:
his barber and a grocer led a cell
of base reactionary types directed
by British and American intel.
He gave us everything we wished to know;
unfortunately, none of it was so.

THE SUICIDE SPEAKS

When I conceived to dangle from the beam,
a plumb bob in the heavy hayseed air,
I thought that I could build upon that dream,
but when the dream came true, I was not there.
Hopeless, my plan had given me a hope
on which to hang my life, that heaving wreck
of ego and despair. So with the rope
I made a simple cradle for my neck.
Hillary knew no greater sense of triumph
on Everest's top than I knew standing high
above the barn's main floor about to jump,
anticipating how I was to die.
But when I leaped, I learned that death was not
the rest I sought, and learning that, forgot.

WALNUTS

We know how they arrive here: squirrels forget
the pantries which they planted in the ground
for sustenance through hard-shelled winter. Yet
the drive within the seed surprises still
as emerald plumes like feathers fan around
us in the garden, gutter, lawn, and sill.

Some we will pull, their inconvenient stations
threatening our order; others we will mow;
still others, sprouting in their choice locations,
or one indifferent from our small perspective,
become a forest at our feet and grow
to consequence by natural directive.

This is the way it is with us, as well:
we squirrel ourselves away as memories
in this mind or in that. Then who can tell
which of our sweet and oily fruit will spear
up to the surface, grow into great trees,
and testify that we once planted there?

In hidden places we have long forgotten,
the kernels buried grow into a wood:
ideas by us broadcast, misbegotten,
return in leaf, unbidden, to remind
each of us what we've done for bad or good—
of everything we've dropped and left behind.

STOPPING WITH OUR DAUGHTERS TO WATCH HORSES

"The popularity of the horse rests, indeed, upon a sound and lasting basis; for bicycles and automobiles are fads of the moment, while the love of the horse is rooted in something which is immutable."
—*Bookman* 13 (July 1901)

We took our daughters biking on a trail
that runs along a little nameless creek
and on the fossil backbone of a rail-
road linking places commerce used to seek.
Halfway to one such place, we stopped beside
a pasture to watch quarter horses graze,
each daughter dreaming of which she would ride
if life were built of other, deeper ways.
What magnetism is it in the horse
attracts these girls as if here were the pole
their hearts had always sought? Why does this force
draw them toward the field of its control?
We watched an hour, then, slaves to how things are,
biked back the way we came to find our car.

WHAT ORPHEUS REMEMBERS

I have tried so hard to remember her:
her eyes, her lips, her feet, her neck, her voice—
that voice I used to say was like the breeze
tickling the beech leaves—but the effort fails.
All has grown dim. My mind is like an oyster,
filtering dark water for debris
from which to reconstruct the past.
So why is it that I remember Hell
so vividly: old Hades's putrid breath,
Persephone's pale breasts,
clatter of bone on rock, songs of the lost?
Perhaps such terrors cannot be forgotten.
Thus I remember how Eurydice
was finally lost, how doubt compelled my turn—
my thoughtless, final turn to her—the cry
she gave as she fell away from me—my name,
low pitched and mournful as my lyre now sounds
to me, vexed as I am with presbycusis—
and her hands, bodiless, reaching out from darkness
like great moths flitting in the night.
My memories flit in gloomy regions now,
Cecropias seeking for that perfect flower
last seen so long ago that it might not—
and this I fear much more than death itself—
be recognized if even it could be found.

OREGON TRAIL

Imaginary bison run
across the yard, a great stampede,
blocking the trail to Oregon
my emigrating daughters need

to follow if they hope to make
a new home in the Willamette
before hard snow. While bison shake
the neighborhood, my daughters fret

about the state of their provisions
and how to keep their powder dry.
They calculate with fine precision
what still remains of their supply

of peanut butter cookies, juice,
and apple wedges in the pack
their mother victualled for their use
this morning. But they won't turn back

no matter what (at least, until
we call them to a meal tonight,
or else until they've had their fill
of cholera and Indian fights).

What myths tomorrow will depend
upon three little girls who play
at pioneers? What they pretend
to be and do this summer day

and days to follow will create
a fable of a golden past,
as children's games and songs inflate
into legends that will last.

After the storm of buffalo,
my daughters cautiously move on,
watching for Sioux, Arapaho,
and Pawnee on the neighbor's lawn.

Their swing set is Fort Laramie.
The girls pause here to rest before
returning to this fantasy
that teaches life in metaphor.

FOR A YOUNG SON FAR FROM HOME

Standing tonight beside your empty crib,
I watch the moon ascend the evening sky.
It is the ball before a medium's face,
shining, but cloudy with uncertainty,
most unrevealing on this clearest night.
It causes me to think about you lying
far away and surrounded in glorious moonlight.
Near death, you are as much like memory
as anyone can be and still have breath.
The teddy bears and rabbits on your bed
hold possibilities and promises
that might come true if but imagination
would make them leap to life. Perhaps you will
return and clear away the dust that covers
everything in this room. Perhaps your laughter
will polish these walls clean of silence again.
Until that time, the moon outside your window
blinds me like the reflection of the sword
God placed before the sacred gates of Eden
to bar our broken parents a return,
and sorrow, licensed by love, pours over me
with the flood of moonlight into your empty room.

CAMPING IN THE RAIN

The rain on the tent fly sounds
like distant footsteps. Perhaps
you have changed your mind
and have sent a messenger to
tell me so. Or
perhaps it is even
you that I hear
coming. You probably
found me gone and,
knowing me as you do, have
followed me up the shoulder of this
mountain. I can almost see you
on the trail, clutching your fragile apology
against your heart
as if it were made of
fine china.
Perhaps it is
even you that I hear. Perhaps,
but no. It is only
rain on the fly of the tent. It is
only the apologetic rain. It
is only distant footsteps which
will always approach, but
never arrive.

PRAYING WITH EMERSON

He spoke about the Oversoul within
all creatures as their animating spark,
the ignorance of which alone is sin,
by knowing which alone one may embark
upon the sea of self-sufficiency
which our transcendent ships must navigate
into that harbor of Divinity
where democratic gods associate.
We listened rapt while he invoked the force,
both immanent and everywhere displayed,
that motivates a libertarian course,
and then we bowed our heads and with him prayed,
each placing ancient faith upon the shelf
to call on God by talking to himself.

YELLOW-EYED GRACKLE

Yellow-eyed grackle,
at dawn your raucous cry,
harsh as a file's scream,
grates against the sky.

It seems a criticism
of the very light.
Perhaps, dark complainer,
you prefer the night

whose flag your feathers are.
Such prejudice is absurd.
Or do you long for death as well,
O midnight-headed bird?

AT THE CHURCH PICNIC

for Nancy

You place our basket on the tabletop
beside the others lined up in a row
like cargo ships at dock. Behind, I stop
to watch as you unload with hands that know

each thing's appointed place: the cups, the plates,
the napkins, spoons, forks, knives, all carefully
assigned their spots. Your guiding eye creates
a chapel for this summer liturgy.

You next erect a sandwich ziggurat
within the polis of the common fare
to dominate its skyline; spread a flat
display of apples, tangerines, grapes, pears,

and strawberries; then summon with a hand
our daughters from the nearby swings. Small birds,
they fly across the grass at your command
and seat themselves with deferential words.

Another child will come this fall, and you,
at twenty-seven weeks, are, like the year,
grown great with all the virtues which accrue
in warm and fruitful seasons. I come near.

You pour fresh lemonade like a libation
into a tumbler, drinking it in sips.
Thirst quenched, your smile serves as an invitation
to taste the citrus lingering on your lips.

TWO SONGS

1. Song of Natural Virtue

Teach me to dance as the molecules
that tangoed in the primal sea,
making together by the rules
of elementary chemistry

organic grace. Or let me sing
the music of the cosmic spheres
that sails upon photonic wing,
illuminating space and years.

Then at my death, come bury me
within the soil of heaven's hill,
and from my bones shall sprout a tree
more great and fair than Yggdrasil.

2. Song of Primary Virtue

Teach me to thrive in the shadow of
a certain death, and grant me grace
to trust the future to your sovereign
providence. Although my race

inherits pride, let me consent
completely to your godly will,
subduing ego to repent
of reigning over Zion's hill

as lord and king. Then when, at last,
I reach the end prescribed for me,
my life, vainglory in the past,
will be your praise eternally.

GENETIC LOAD

Our atavistic attributes
will dog us to our dying days,
confounding efforts to confute
occult hereditary ways.

Parents from generations back
bequeathed to me a mixed estate
of enzymatic wealth and lack,
assuring my genetic fate.

Which ancestor from ages gone
first wore the features of my face?
What poor progenitor passed on
perfectionism without grace?

With whom did my insecurity
originate? Whose green, weak eyes
were given as a gift to me
without a tag? What compromise

of dominant and recessive genes
kept them from being brown or blue?
Will any nurture contravene
the laws of nature braided through

our DNA? No. None remake
their origins. The family gnomes
cannot be lost, will not forsake
their lodging in our chromosomes.

PASCAL'S GOOD NIGHT

My Jacqueline has gone, and I'll soon follow—
death is the only goal all must pursue;
this world's a bubble, slippery and hollow;
your gravity draws me from it to you.
Collecting years is meaningless distraction:
both thirty-nine and ninety come to nought
as numerators hovering in a fraction
above infinity. Thus I've not sought
vain comfort from the surgeon or physician,
but, wagering on you, bow to the pain
your providence decrees as my condition:
be near now, Lord, that losing life bring gain,
as losing vision may give second sight.
Then I will see how darkness leads to light.

CICERO COMMENTS

1. On Searching Syracuse for Archimedes's Tomb

On streets as narrow as a Gallic mind,
I wandered through the city and inquired
of every ancient Greek where I could find
the mausoleum where they had interred
that architect and fulcrum of their fame:
old Archimedes who, in reverie,
was slain by my coarse countryman who came
and proved a point with trigonometry
disguised as steel. At last, I found his tomb
wrapped in a shroud of brambles, briars, and weeds,
the laurels of obscurity or blame
rather than fit memorial to great deeds.
And there I learned there is no ratio
inscribing genius in an afterglow.

2. On the Pleasures of the Garden

Here in converging twilights, let me rest.
While day ebbs slowly westward out to sea
and gathers hope with which it will invest
tomorrow's dawn, may heaven's tranquility
fall with the shadows from the myrtle bough
stretched like beatitude above my head,
and Zeno and his brothers tell me how
to persevere these dark hours without dread.
The scents of mint, bay, cypress, oleander,
and rose still waft through this gymnasium
despite aspirants after Alexander
who've taken Rome in turn. In Tusculum,
the sunsets and the gardens are so fine
we almost doubt republican decline.

3. On Writing His *Cato the Elder*

The skill it takes to make a specious claim
wrapped in the toga of an ancient's words
to cloak its incredulity with fame
shows rhetoric both skillful and absurd.
Such argument is best if not profound
or tightly logical, but rather flows
digressively in order that the sound
of language drape what logic would disclose.
I hoped in writing *De senectute*
to cure the fear of death that all contract,
treating with Xenophon's philosophy
of golden-laureled age to come. In fact,
if winter really looked so good from fall,
there would have been no need to write at all.

4. His Last Oration

I see them coming down the path like hounds
invigorated by the scent of prey.
I've struggled to escape and made the rounds
from shore to ship to shore but cannot stay
this game's end any longer. Put the litter
under that knobby pine where I can wait
for death in peaceful shade. I would not fritter
this final time away in vain debate.
Young Caesar cast me out into this dark
new world where dogs that pant for Anthony
pursue, and now so close I hear them bark.
I'll meet them here. You, soldier! Look to me!
To kill a senator as if a stoat
is base! But do it well. Here is my throat.

DIABETES MELLITUS

The kidney's gold, contaminated, sweet;
blood like molasses, sludging in the feet;

nerves slowly pickled beyond the touch of pain;
the plegic penis that pines to rise again;

eyes entangled in tentacles of red
vessels like fishes clutched by ravenous squid;

lungs haunted by a ghostly, fruity breath—
prevenient spirit of a sticky death:

sugar kills slowly, sweetening us part by part
until, at last, we die of a candied heart.

DROUGHT BREAKER

Two years of drought seem broken by a deluge
that would be the wrath of God were it not mercy.
No doubt some prophet has spoken to Heaven for us
and obtained a grace sufficient to wash away
all memory of withered crops, clear skies, dry wells,
and the taste and texture of dust in the teeth. No wonder
men dance naked in the streets and sing,
and women braid their hair with mint and daisies.
No wonder children clap their hands and laugh
at the tattoo of the downpour on the rooftops.
But may God spare us profligate relief.
For rain may cause the wisest to forget
the vast, dry tragedy of the time behind us,
the unknown danger in the years ahead.

LIKE BALAAM

Thwarted on my journey,
like Balaam past, I wait
upon this narrow road to go
as God should indicate

through some persistent angel.
But I cannot see thrones,
dominions, powers, or princes
with human eyes alone.

And as I have no donkey
possessing second sight
to apprehend such heavenly beings
and turn to left or right

as heaven would direct,
it seems that I must find
a talking ass somewhere to tell
me what is on God's mind.

GOING HOME

The moon rolls out late over the
sleeping contours of central Indiana.
Its light bathes me as I sit in
the belly of the bus, waiting to be regurgitated
as Jonah waited in the fish. Hours
rise like mist from the dark plains,
their fluid regularity punctuated only
by the fitful shadows of
passing woods, the dull lights
of quiet towns and farmsteads, the
barely discernible ghosts
of telephone poles streaking east. I close
my eyes and curl into myself.
Tomorrow is soon, near Chicago.
In my sleep another moon
rises, chaste and lovely, while
the bus's teeth gnash, its ribs rattle, and
I float west in the darkness toward home.

UNCLE HENRY AND THE VIRGIN

When as an old man, Henry Adams took
his afternoon excursions in the park,
he did not take an academic book
along to keep him company till dark.

Instead, his landau drives provided joy
because he took them with a sympathetic
female companion whom he had employed
to keep his soul in touch with the poetic.

The light would drip from yellow poplar trees
and splash on horses, carriage, and the two
who, seated on its cushions, knees to knees,
conversed the hours to life as evening grew.

More than a quarter century had passed
since Clover Adams took the cyanide
that quenched her mortal thirst, her role miscast
as Henry's spouse, although beatified

in Henry's memory. Later, he would choose
another woman for his inspiration,
an object of domestic billets-doux
and Beatrice to love's imagination,

though someone else's wife estranged, and far
from comfort on cold nights. As their years passed,
she thought of Adams as avuncular
instead of amatory, and, at last,

she cast his cautious heart away. But when
in 1912 Aileen Tone sang trouvère
songs in Henry's parlor, he began
to find a counterpoise for his despair.

Miss Tone was only thirty-four and he,
past seventy, expected soon to die.
With virtue captive to necessity,
December sought no romance with July.

Old Adams was her "uncle," she his "niece,"
though readings, rides, and evening conversations
were avenues where Adams found surcease
from what were more than fatherly frustrations.

Thus paired platonically, they went along,
albeit Henry never could disguise
his joy when she would sing some old French song,
his admiration for her dancing his eyes.

One fear, however, haunted Henry's mind:
he understood the natural desire
of chilly bones for heat, but could not find
a reason ice should fascinate a fire.

HONEY WAGON

Somewhere ahead
along this road,
a manure spreader
sows a load

which angers eyes
and troubles nose.
The refuse flies.
I quickly close

my dash vents, though
defense is vain,
for I have no
power to maintain

a steady state
against the ghosts
that permeate
organic hosts.

Confetti-like
straw dung that's thrown
upon the pike
turns cobblestone.

As I deploy
my Camry over
this corduroy
recycled clover,

I cough and swear
at cow pies, chaff,
and poison air,
but after, laugh.

For God has wit:
so we must go
on spreading shit
to make things grow.

THE YOUNG WIDOW BRAIDS HER DAUGHTER'S HAIR

She still gets out of bed at half past six,
rising to make her daughter in first grade
orange juice to go with Cheerios and fix
the little girl's brown hair into a braid.
She starts by gently brushing through the swell
that surges wildly on her child's small head,
and, disciplining this, smoothes out, as well,
the wave in her own Fundy tide of dread.
Each day this helps a morning hour go by:
some sea is parted with her daughter's hair,
and heart less heavy while her fingers fly,
she weaves a rope that lifts her from despair.
For that short time, life seems much as before,
except, of course, he won't come through the door.

MISSISSIPPI RHINOCEROS

An alternative history of the drowning of Old Put, as leaked to the *Dubuque Herald* by the publicity manager for the Dan Rice Circus

One August night in 1861,
some nineteen river miles below La Crosse,
the packet boat *Key City*, on its run
home to Dubuque, collided with the Dan
Rice circus steamer. No great harm was done
to either vessel, though Rice bore the loss
of a highly valued, trained rhinoceros
who, caged, fell in the river, where no man

could hope to save him, and then disappeared
into the indifference of the night
without a groan or bubble. It was feared
the animal had drowned. But tragedy
will pay no bills, and so the circus veered
off to its port of next engagement, right
in the channel, with a floating bight
of rope left like a memorial in its lee.

The rhino, being erudite had read
or heard that iron bars could never make
a cage, however, so he used his head
to ram the door from his presumptive cell,
and fled the Mississippi's muddy bed,
but turned the wrong way in the packet's wake,
to left, an understandable mistake
given the way that his apartment fell.

Days later in Dubuque, a clerk was walk-
ing on the Mississippi wharf and spied
beyond the steamboats nuzzled at the dock
the wayward rhino battling the chain
that fixed the harbor buoys. Men used the block
and tackle on a dredger to provide
the beast its rescue and then notified
the circus of its providential gain.

I have been told that I should never look
for zebras when the sound of hooves is near.
But things don't always happen by the book
of numbers, nor are all events reprise.
A rhino hanging like a grappling hook
from buoys chained to a wharf boat is a clear
miracle, telling us to persevere
against all odds, though every chance denies.

But we know this redaction is untrue.
We know Old Put (that was the rhino's name)
did not escape the river to pursue
another season doing tricks and dance,
but drowned unceremoniously. So you
and I must choose between one mythic claim
to glory and another. Both bring fame,
though death, I think, deficient in romance.

WALKING THE DEAD END TOGETHER IN LATE AUTUMN

Oaks trickle skyward like meandering tears
defining channels on a mourner's face.
Immobile, they have cried this way for years
in stubborn, solid sorrow. Absent grace,
we, too, are firmly rooted into place—

this place where dead grass scratches at the air
and streams of sunlight slowly filter down
over abandoned fields and gardens, where
time melts residual colors into brown—
the muddy hue in which all colors drown.

On limbs above us, crows converse. Their voices,
more cutting than November breezes, seem
to mock attempts to remake April's choices
and find some present that past might redeem.
We crush dry leaves like desiccated dreams

with almost every step we take toward where
this old road ends a course it can't explain—
as if its future vanished in gray air,
as if it were a song without refrain—
and then we turn and go back home again.

SNOW-BLIND

Snow like a silence long desired
embraces each branch and remnant leaf
within this wood, disguising tired
browns in a silver lattice. Grief

is a rationally muted emotion in
such crystalline beauty sharp and bright:
eyes grown acute with sorrow begin
to fail of vision in such light.

A NEW MOTHER IN SPARTA

I climbed the bright and stony trail each day
for forty weeks as hope grew in my womb,
threading through groves of cypress, fig, and bay
to reach Therapne's top and Helen's tomb.
There I would supplicate the lovely shade
of Sparta's queen to grant my unborn child
the boon of beauty she herself displayed,
cuckolding husbands, driving women wild
with envy holly-sharp. A plane tree stands
outside my window. Holiest to she
whom I invoke, its leaves outstretched like hands
were promise of beatitude to me.
A handsome daughter sucks now at my breast
and vindicates my faith. Old ways are best.

EVER AFTER

This is the way their fairy tale has ended:
Charming grown old, the princess bride a hag;
with love secured and virtue well defended,
she found him a fool, he her a nag.
Together long years, their lives became mundane
and bitter. They cursed bowels, backs, and hearts
and whined of faithless friends. Could love remain
while men and functions failed them? By what arts
of evil sorcery did they come to age:
eyes grown opaque, joints stiff, skin like old leather,
and even the mind's wings withered? What foul rage
brought them to this, their evermore, together?
As newlyweds they thought it certain truth
that mythic ending guaranteed them youth.

SOMEDAY

Someday when there is nothing we must do,
the oriole will sing once more, the pine
will sway within the sighing breeze, and you
and I will sip the summer hours like wine.

But present obligation cannot be
denied, and now the oriole has flown
this wood. The pine bough stirs uneasily
above your empty chair. I drink alone.

EARLY GIRLS

My daughters cradle life within their hands:
tomato transplants just six inches high.
Each girl, though green and young, well understands
the plant she holds is, like a butterfly,

a fragile creature, needing every care
to settle in the garden and take root
in earth—there, hopefully, to grow and bear,
in season due, a bumper crop of fruit.

I guide each daughter's winglike hands with mine
until the 'Early Girls' are in the ground,
then watch my girls flush scarlet with condign
joy in the new vocation that they've found.

An older neighbor working in his yard
stops raking to address me: "It's an art
to garden well, and, though the work is hard,
crops turn out best when nurtured from the start."

PLATE TECTONICS

When wandering tectonic plates collide,
and continental shelves meet and embrace,
two are made one, but as when words elide,
are imperfect in their union. Face-to-face,

fault lines arise where lands communicate
their passion to each other with most force:
in intimacy, both would dominate,
leading to friction all along their course.

Contentions that erupt around these faults
should not surprise, for love brings seismic shifts
to lovers' lives, drops valleys, and exalts
plains into mountains where the bedrock lifts

and buckles under pressure from another's
expectations. So the Alps were born:
when Africa sought Europe for its lover,
their glorious quarrel raised the Matterhorn.

As we merge together, we are pressed
into new conformations never known
alone, by geothermal powers stressed
like rock and water under Yellowstone

until we quake and fracture. Then erupting
with pent volcanic violence, we pour
our anger over everything, corrupting
all around us, as each tries to score

a victory by which one may achieve
some dominance, not so much in accord
as resignation, though the conflict grieve
us both and change the face of its reward.

But as our crusty continents compete,
we earn a compensation none deny
when charcoal turns to diamond in our heat
and Himalayas vault into the sky.

MUSKELLUNGE CREEK

Grant County, Wisconsin
Answering a California visitor's question: "Where are the fish?"

Though some, fooled by the name, may come to look
for muskies here and hope to get a try
at one, none ever swam within this brook
cartographers have labeled with a lie.
Perhaps this name was but some farmer's wish
to flee his cows and crops and find a place,
green and reedy, where he, like a fish,
might safely hide. So seen, there's no disgrace
in this misnomer, just a fantasy—
desire unrealistically projected
onto a shallow creek too small to be
that hope's fulfillment—not the truth neglected.
Facts cause imagination no duress:
none look for angels in Los Angeles.

PHILANTHROPIST

He loves mankind, but only as abstraction:
the real particulars hold no attraction.

MATERIALISM SIMPLY EXPLAINED

The laws of nature, never being lenient,
allow love to be merely supervenient.

THE DEATH OF JAMES THE JUST

Eusebius, *History of the Church* 2.23.4

When James the Just was placed
atop the temple wall,
the curious made haste
to see the righteous fall.

A crowd, with faces raised
like shields against the sun,
stood transfixed and amazed
beneath the bastion

where Sadducees and scribes
traduced James's filial God
with hostile diatribes.
Some listening applauded,

but most had stopped to make
this day relief from others,
and didn't have a take
on James and God as brothers.

For them, this was pure art,
and, although truth might be
as red as blood, the part
was all they came to see

and hear. So while they ate
their olives, dates, and bread,
they bet on what awaited
the ancient church's head.

James claimed in his confession
Christ would return some hour
now imminent from session
at Yahweh's hand of power,

a claim that did not please
the elders, who then vowed
to cast him to the breeze
and make him ride the cloud.

Thus James was finally thrown
down from the parapet
and set upon with stone
on stone to meet regret.

At this the crowd began
to fracture like a shell;
some justified the man
while others wished him hell.

The latter hope seemed filled
(despite a Rechabite's
brave protest) when they killed
the godly Nazirite

with fuller's club: at last,
dispatching with one blow
the Christ's enthusiast
and those there for the show.

DAPHNE

Divine Apollo thought he could presume
the right to plant his flag on any hill
and take possession of a fertile womb
as he desired, regardless of her will.
One day while I was hunting in the woods
for deer, Apollo got the drop on me,
but I appealed before he took the goods
and was transformed into a laurel tree.
Now I no longer party with the nymphs,
or wander Thessaly for novel sights,
and never touch—though sometimes I can glimpse—
my river-father. Still, I like my rights.
A god who swears eternal love deceives:
some fates are worse than growing bark and leaves.

VIGIL FOR A SICK SON

The moon tiptoes into your room as if trying not to wake you.
White as a nurse, it sweeps to your side, adjusts
blankets with a flick of shadows, runs
deft fingers across your feverish forehead.
We have seen it before. Tonight is routine:
the celestial face checks
each pump, each tube, each monitor in succession, then
passes from the room, leaving only
a ghost of light for us to watch you by.

Why is everything in this hospital black or white?
The yeast salted in your lungs and spleen, the cells
invading your marrow with brilliance,
the blankets on your bed, the walls, the moon, the night:
such things have blinded us to the color you
have been without so long.
Still, though cones have atrophied from disuse and pupils
grown large, we continue to watch you, grateful
for even the comfort of pallid light.

But it is small comfort.
As the last lunar radiance slips from these walls, we
are engulfed in amebic darkness.
We tread its protoplasm anxiously, dazzled
by the brightness of tragedy, and
pray as we struggle that some great flash
will not finally come and
carry you far away,
beyond our skills in love's resuscitation.

LENIN

It's late. He walks the lonely corridor
in this part of the Kremlin with his cat
hammocked in his arm. He stops before
the door of every commissariat
that's still aglow and enters into each,
although he knows the commissars have gone.
Frugality is something he must teach:
he switches off the lights that they've left on.
He's like the cat he strokes so tenderly;
both have strong preferences, but weak affections.
His true love is an ideology
of which both wife and mistress are reflections.
At last, he finds the final burning light
and turns it off, inviting in the night.

NEBUCHADNEZZAR RESTORED

Returned from animal madness, can he tell
them of the throbbing passion at his throat,
the force that choked the words he knew so well
and killed his human music note by note?

How will he convey the depth of anguish
that once he launched upon a primal cry
through sounds and signs and syntax of a language
abstract and pure? Prehension may defy

the power of noun and predicate to enslave,
the power of imperative to express.
This he has learned, and now, though others rave
effusively, he values language less.

So, taciturn, his speech more sleek, more spare,
he ponders the untranslatable thoughts of beast
still also his, and rules with oxlike stare
and canine jaw at altar, court, and feast.

Though man again, he still lives bestial years,
and when his courtiers come on him too soon
some early dawns, they cover eyes and ears,
aghast to find him baying at the moon.

STEALING PEARS

Augustine, *Confessions* 2.4.9

Iniquity, O Lord, will be delicious:
always in season, always tender, sweet,
blushing, and aromatic. Not capricious,
it always hangs low, begging us to eat.
One night, I stripped the neighbors' tree of pears—
not Grade A pears, but seconds grown for swine—
taking them not because the fruit was theirs,
nor yet because I wanted it for mine.
The only flavor in the act was sin
itself, in which we ever hope to gain
that lie the serpent promised Eve she'd win
by holding your commandment in disdain.
But as my hands grew sticky with crime's dew,
your hand, O Lord, was pulling me toward you.

RABBIT AND COYOTE

Held frozen in its place
by foreign hunger near,
the rabbit plans for flight
while grinding on its fear.
It tries to time the race
for its escape just right:
the coyote will chase—
forbid that it should bite.

The coyote must wait
to strike propitiously,
by care and cunning choose
(but expeditiously)
its timing, for if late
or early it will lose
the game and will not sate
its hunger with excuse.

We usually cheer the hare,
though our default position
is that of carnivore,
and hunting is our mission.
For in the end, our care
for weaker things is poor:
it vanishes in air
when want is at the door.

THE GHOST OF DR. C. SARGENT FERRIS DEFENDS HIMSELF

"Where my marvelous Vital Life Fluid is used, no disease can exist, for it is the secret of life—life itself."
—Dr. C. Sargent Ferris, *A Friend of Womankind: Diseases of Women and How to Cure Them* (Cleveland, 1903)

Knowing the time was short, that chance would pass
forever like the bison from the plains,
and sympathizing with the desperate mass
of women stung by neurasthenic pains

and female ailments, in 1903
I marketed the sages' magic stone,
the only universal remedy
that ever was, or ever will be, known—

old aqua vitae, labeled Vital Life—
and fortified it with the pleasant taste
of cherry cordial. Good for mother, wife,
sister, or daughter, there would be no waste

in any order, and the price would reach
even the worker's purse, egality
a virtue in the market. Then to teach
the lost this gospel comprehensively,

I came out with an illustrated tract.
Its science gave my argument the air
of credibility. Equipped with fact,
a patient might in confidence compare

my treatment to all others. I believed
(and still believe) that what I sold was light,
a light I could not hide. If I deceived
in trivials, in motive, I was right.

Your knowledge is not virtue, after all.
Why should your science castigate my art?
My fascination's old: you may recall
a little wine makes glad a heavy heart.

The times were different too. I didn't know
what you know now, though I'll admit it's true
we said more than we knew, but to bestow
hope to the hopeless, more than truth is due.

Hyperbole may wear an angel's face
and, like an angel to those in distress,
be mediator of supernal grace,
whether veracity be more or less.

Distilling and decocting into hope
from language an elixir to make whole
the broken proves me twice a philanthrope,
physician both to body and to soul.

The Vital Life I sold was really not
that fluid I so named, but something more:
an object fit for faith was what they sought,
and that is what they gave their money for.

And if I made a little on the way,
the Good Book says a prophet earns his dime.
Success has costs an owner must defray,
and being sharp in business is no crime.

Accuse me not of being insincere.
I own no guilt and won't apologize
for making women's comfort my career,
nor for the benefits that come from lies.

RUINS

Pill bottles in assorted sizes lie
scattered across the smooth Formica plain
of the bathroom countertop. They testify,
like pediments and pillars that remain—

broken, askew, and fallen—on the site
of some great ancient temple, to a past
both glorious and vivid, and invite
the meditations of elegiasts.

The architect of this Asklepion
built carefully that it might stand for years.
Its private altar, visited each dawn
and dusk, suppressed his pain and muffled fears.

But understanding some theology,
we realize that this temple's final fall
was foreordained, despite the care that he
spent on the cornerstone that bore it all.

MEMORANDUM FROM WADI KERITH

At God's command I fled to Kerith Brook,
leaving the royal anger in the dust
stirred up by sin and drought, that none might look
and find a word of hope in which to trust.
The ravens bring me ibex twice a day,
and bread, sometimes with olives, dates, or cheese,
and there are no distractions when I pray:
a prophet should have only Heaven to please.
The weather will stay dry in consequence
of Ahab's marriage to that loose Phoenician
whose ideology gives God offense,
though satisfying every politician.
So Israel's government belongs to knaves,
while Yahweh's prophets hide themselves in caves.

GRAND ARMY

Now run your fingers through my thinning hair.
Enroll with ease the remnant of that corps
which guarded once my capital with care,
and sigh for veterans who are no more.

True patriots, again they feel the call
to duty, though their ranks be old and few,
and so they muster, at attention all,
in order to commend my cause to you.

WHAT PTOLEMY KNEW

"Mortal as I am, I know that I am born for a day, but when I follow the serried stars in their circular course, my feet no longer touch the earth."
—Ptolemy of Alexandria

Tired of this up and down, this never certain
trip of all trips, without known proximate
destination (though ultimate is sure),
I seek for where, by prophetic indication,
I might repose my head on stone and dream
of a stairway to heaven or follow oracular stars.
In such a place of vision, even the least
of constellations dance, their points of light
as beautiful as the sparkling eyes of deer.
There, gaze held by clarity of sight,
my feet would grow hard, toes coalesce, and I
would walk the earth no more, but bound through skies
thick with star-jeweled antlers, hooves of fire,
seeking in the glory of the starlit night
an intimation of that immortal wood.

THAT OCTOBER MORNING

I still remember that October morning.
Sunlight dripped down on us from
red leaves, and the cold air
knotted our breaths between us.
You touched my face as if it were an
old postcard and kissed me—
your eyelashes wet as morning
leaves, your lips
redder than the leaves.
Then you walked away.
My blood poured after you, leaving
me dry as a rope, and
the maples bled into the sky.

LOSS OF LIGHT

I must have pushed you too high; Heaven seen,
no beauty of mortal earth or sky could then
compete for your mind's allegiance, your heart's affection.
So you left us, and now your swing is empty
except for the pallid bones of memory.
But how insubstantial those bones really are!
Could it be that everything about you
was no more real than our dreams for your future were?
No, you were with us once; your absence now
confirms your presence then. I don't know how
to explain this paradox, except to say
that we know when a star goes out by how the night
seems doubly dark for loss of its precious light.

CHRISTMAS CAROLING IN COLONIAL WILLIAMSBURG

Many here know only a single verse
of any given carol, sometimes less—
sometimes an isolated phrase or terse
refrain like "Gloria." Most still confess

the apostolic faith, though as naïve
in its theology as those days when
as children they would sing on Christmas Eve
in church. Now with the season come again,

and in this antique place, they try to find
a renaissance of meaning in such words
and build significance from what they've mined
in scraps and shards of songs heard and reheard:

a reconstruction of that first Noel
the angel said on Christmas night, how God
gave rest to gentlemen, or why go tell
of Christ's birth everywhere. Still, these seem odd

ideas to but a few, quaint like remains
of stoneware bottles or ceramic ware—
not ancient verities belief sustains,
but artifacts dug from some basement here.

DÉNOUEMENT

His life in ruin at its end
(as all must be, though we pretend
it's otherwise), the single word
that was Kane's last was barely heard,

swaddled in the wheeze of death.
Men analyzed Kane's final breath
as if his whisper were the key
to unlock years of mystery.

They spent long hours looking for
some secret project, paramour,
or partner, although none was found.
Still, after Kane was in the ground,

the speculation only grew,
but no one guessed at what was true:
the final fever in Kane's head
had been about a burning sled.

NANCY AFTER HER BATH

Naked except for hairpins and a book,
she lingers at the door to let me look
upon her form in full, a welcome grace
this early hour allows. Perhaps her face,
though comely, would not launch ten thousand ships,
but mine, at least, is driven by those lips
and by those eyes which, as I watch, watch me
with more than casual curiosity.

The pages of the book she leafs through dance
beneath her fingertips' insouciance
like flames within a draft: a signal fire
drawing me toward the altar of desire.
She fans this blaze while love's intentions rise,
then to a question never posed, replies,
"At times like this, a book's the thing to wear,
if it's good enough," and, this said, drops her hair.

ORANGES

Columbus held the world within his hand
when he saw a sail-winged butterfly appear
on the orange's horizon like a reprimand
to the wafer earth. Considering that sphere

of citrus as a planet in his mind,
he set himself to comprehend the way
to east from west, through western seas to find
the heavenly khan, the riches of Cathay

and Calicut. An error, but from this
America was accidentally born,
and Ocean's dread and bestial abyss
made rational from Iceland to Cape Horn.

The grace which made analogy between
an orange and planet fruitful may inspire
our minds to see the unseen in the seen
and guide us to the Indies we desire

or even unknown shores. Now when I peel
my morning orange, I scrutinize its skin
for any providence God may reveal
of unknown continents yet left to win.

EDWARD HICKS: *AN INDIAN SUMMER VIEW OF THE FARM AND STOCK OF JAMES C. CORNELL, 1848*

Although it's topographical, this scene
still seems ethereal, as if the horses,
sheep, cattle, pigs, and men were caught between
mundane things and the angels in their courses.
The livestock, loosed from stanchion and from stall,
crowd foreground in millennial expectation,
waiting serenely for the trump's last call.
Behind them, farmers, rapt in conversation,
inhabit pastures green. Peripherally,
a ploughman drives his team, but stirs no dust;
fat haystacks fade into eternity;
and thin trees cling to leaves of gold and rust.
This painted world is too good to believe.
Perhaps that's why the style is called naïve.

A SUPPLICATION

Weak in faith, O Lord, as dull in sight,
I cry to you for spectacles and light
sufficient for myopic saints as I
to see your glory pouring from the high
throne of Heaven and filling earth with grace.
Or if I must be sightless, let me trace
your tracings in my book of life with fingers
sensitive and skilled in the appropriate Braille
and contemplate with mind that looks and lingers
not upon my weakness, but your strength.
Then in that moment when again I fail—
as fail I will, possessed of doubled mind—
to celebrate your faithfulness, at length
turn me, O Christ, and, though completely blind,
let me see
your sacrifice upon that ancient tree
for me.

SIXTH STREET WHARF

Washington, DC, June 1864
After Cold Harbor

At the Sixth Street Wharf, the soldiers disembark,
the savvy boys who bought their way from hell
by bribing death with arm or leg. The ark
that bore them home rocks gently on the swell-
ing river at high tide. Red in the light
of dusk's fast-failing lantern, stacks and spars
like specters of limbs absent haunt this night
inhabited by regiments of stars.
Behind the purple wounded come the dead,
boxed and anonymous in gray parade,
no general riding glorious at their head,
no martial music marching them to shade.
But redeploying to a new position,
they'll faithfully fulfill their final mission.

MY FATHER'S OAKS

On summer evenings when I was a boy,
my dad would sometimes load us in the car—
a fifty-four Bel Air—and drive for joy
down old Route Six to one particular

bur oak grove, the homestead of his heart,
perched on a little swale of glacial loam.
We'd turn into the lane as if to part
a sea of dropseed, turkeyfoot, and brome,

but stop within the shallows. Dad would turn
the Chevy's engine off, and we would roll
our windows down, the better to discern
the distant corn-fletched fields as late mists stole

up from the river like a blanket drawn
by unseen hands; to watch as distant trees
flamed and sputtered till their light was gone;
to listen to the murmuring of bees

feasting on black-eyed Susan, spurge and vetch;
to smell the sweet aroma of cut hay
like hazelnuts and almonds; and to catch
thrushes and doves petitioning the day

to never end. Meanwhile the bur oaks stood
like Abrahams turned heavenward in prayer,
perpetually beseeching that God should
remember all the good he'd planted there.

Except to tell us where the house should be,
my dad said very little to us here,
but let the opening's doxology
and benediction work on eye and ear.

We'd stay until the red and fattened sun
rolled up the light that trailed its going down,
then pull back on the highway, visit done,
and drive the seven miles back into town.

My father never realized his goal
of country life. No dream coerces pity
from providence; our hopes do not control
all circumstance. He died young in the city.

As seasons passed, my memory of Dad's oak
woodland was buried under littered leaves,
the depth of feeling it could once evoke
lost in forgetful mold. But mind deceives.

What hibernates may suddenly revive
if some surprising spring should rise, and so
sprout from its dormancy as much alive
as ever it had been long years ago.

I now live half a state away from where
my father pondered life within the shade-
and-sunlight tartan underneath a bur
oak canopy and haven't seen his glade

in decades. Then while on the road last week,
the June day draining slowly from the sky,
I stumbled on a wood I almost took
for praying trees, and slowed as I passed by.

I briefly thought I saw my father's old
car at the understory's edge, but when,
with shifting light, my reverie went cold,
I woke up in the present once again.

I drove back home with past associations
revived and found that I could not forget
bur oaks raised up like silent invocations.
I'll go by there again and may stop yet.

PRENUPTIAL COUNSEL

He or she who would avoid all strife
should never take, nor ever be, a wife.

ALONE IN NOVEMBER ABOVE LOCK AND DAM NUMBER 11

Here seagulls stitch the gray and grainy sky
to the Mississippi River, but this seam
of heaven to earth seems loosely joined, and I
fear it may sunder under the extreme
pressure exerted by some windy gust
and fly like a sail torn from its spars, to be
never more seen, a roof forever lost,
reprising in its fate our history.
A week ago, the Indian summer gold
reflected from the reservoir, but then
the weather changed, and with it, you grew cold
and left. The seagulls make their loops again.
As feared, the thread won't hold—clouds flap away.
Beneath the dam, the river turns to spray.

GRASS WILL FIND THE SMALLEST CRACK

Grass will find the smallest crack
within a sidewalk or a street
to plant itself where any lack
of resolution plagues concrete.

Foxtail and fescue, crab and rye
invade such deserts to create
in every space they occupy
oases of a greener state.

By their example taught, I must
then find some crevice in your heart
where wear and water pile up dust
that root can make a hopeful start.

DRIVE-THRU

On early weekday mornings, she awaits
his coming with high school anticipation,
although she's thirty-six. He always states
his order like a perfect peroration:
an orange juice and a sandwich stratified
with sausage, egg, and cheddar. He smiles when
he pays her, and she feels their souls elide
the moment that they both possess the ten.
When giving change she sometimes lets her hand
linger above his like a weary tern
or petrel hovering over hoped-for land
it will not touch for fear what it might learn.
Then he departs without more thought of her,
and she must greet another customer.

MOONRISE

It ascends the sky slowly,
a slice of peach, a
gold florin
half-buried in
azure dust,
Saint-Gaudens's
Diana of the Tower
balanced
upon the curve
of one
long
leg.

CORRUPTED BEARS

"WARNING! Corrupted bears in area"
—Legend on a sign near Estes Park, Colorado

When lacking human sponsors, bears will earn
a decent living working in the woods.
Omnivorous and diligent, they spurn
nothing that's edible of nature's goods.

They feed as well on beetle grubs and bees
as acorns, hazelnuts, and huckleberries;
and carrion chance of squirrel or deer will please
their palates just as jay's eggs and black cherries.

But honest bears are getting hard to find.
Our garbage cans are like bear smorgasbords,
the patronage of which has redefined
bears' psyches such that many now are wards

of man's misgovernment. The free ice cream,
old cheese, stale enchiladas, past-ripe fruit,
and bits of pastries are an ursine dream
of social justice realized. This loot

so easily obtained is fast replacing
instinctive struggle with efficiency,
as bears line up to eat, each bite erasing
old memories of self-sufficiency.

Utopians complain that every past
is bound in primitive, primeval night
with day unknown, but brightest days will cast
the deepest shadows with their glaring light.

Historically, bears here are not malicious
and shyly stay away from humankind,
but unearned wealth has made them more capricious,
and some have entered houses, hot to find

a sandwich or a sugar plum to eat.
For now, they think of what's yours as their oyster,
and when confronted, they will not retreat
to past austerity in nature's cloister.

Toward former labors, bears are reticent
due to the ease of accessing our stash,
considering it bear entitlement
to raid our picnics, pantries, tents, and trash.

We euthanize recalcitrants at plunder
that children may play safely in the park,
although this rends a heaven-on-earth asunder
and forces bears to forage in the dark.

WHY I PLANT REDBUDS

"If I knew that tomorrow was the end of the world,
I would plant an apple tree today."
—Attributed, probably incorrectly, to Martin Luther

Whether he really owns the aphorism,
or it belongs to someone else instead
(perhaps it's a rabbinic witticism),
it sounds like something Luther might have said.
He understood that Yahweh had designed
Adam to be both gardener and priest
in order that humanity would find
work sacred every day, no labor least.
Earth creaks and wobbles on its ancient axis;
it always seems as if we're near the end.
Now is our opportunity for praxis;
in planting redbud trees, I comprehend
how more time than I have, I cannot borrow,
and that one day, there will be no tomorrow.

LOVERS' LEAP

Vernon County, Wisconsin

Five hundred feet above the Mississippi—
its waters indigo, purple, and brown,
changeable and oily as starling's
feathers in the sun—
we are surprised by peace as if by
a rare flower unexpectedly discovered.
It is not just the pungent exuberance of the goat prairie—
the groundsel and turkeyfoot, the
dropseed, alumroot, and coneflower,
the fleabane daisy
and chicory—that sets us at ease. Nor
is it only the proud oak and hickory tangled
behind us, nor the
dark and tenacious cedars springing
like Mithraic incarnations from
dolomite cliffs and talus.
It is not merely
the gulls peeling the sky overhead and
dropping rinds of heaven like manna from
their perfect wings, nor the egrets feeding
like nits on the river's sleek skin.
It is not even the summer sun, bright and
optimistic as a voyageur's smile.
But it is the river itself—
the great river flexing through the
continent and
pouring America into the
wide and distant gulf—

that has won us.
It opens its broad heart to us and
calls us, saying, "Children. Children,
be at rest." The Mississippi
courts us tenderly and whispers,
"Let it happen. I will hold you."
We listen, and we tell ourselves
that it is not so terribly far, that
the wind will carry us down gently,
that the water is beautiful and
our feet heavy,
and we think one could,
one almost could,
jump from here.

THE DAY THE RAIN BEGAN

Genesis 7:12

Today seemed just an ordinary day.
The sun rose like an irritated eye;
wives cooked rice pancakes; children went to play
at tag in dusty fields or caught frogs by
the banks of the Euphrates; while the men
took to the brick kilns, potters' wheels, and plows;
lovers arose to make love once again;
and old men at the gate weighed claims and vows.
But now this afternoon, things have grown tense.
Anxiety, abrasive as the sand
of Aram, fills our hearts as we watch dense
cloud ziggurats grow tall above the land,
and weather warnings in cuneiform
alert us of a coming thunderstorm.

PASTERNAK, 1956

I draw long from my stumpy cigarette,
then crush it in the secretary's tray.
The butt is like my hope, and my regret
like smoke that from the ashes trails away.
The secretary smiles. His wolfish jaw
is strong enough to snap a poet's bone.
I silently accept the people's law
as if I were an unplugged microphone.
I knew my book could not be published where
the ghost of Stalin wanders the bazaar,
and men still haunted by that doctrinaire
spirit proscribe all but the crimson star.
The state would swallow artists, soul and skill;
so politicians circle for the kill.

WATCHING TELEVISION COVERAGE OF THE FIRE AT NOTRE DAME DE PARIS, APRIL 15, 2019

A single spark is all it took to seed
the fatal fronds and tendrils of the fire
that now insinuates itself to feed
on ancient wood of transept, nave, and spire—
the boards of fifty acres. Windows burst,
and stained glass falls like petals from a rose.
While firemen work to quench the inferno's thirst,
a crowd awaits what tragedy will expose.
The blaze illumines soul as well as face:
one weeping woman on the street says she
is irreligious, skeptical of grace,
truth, providence, and even history.
Like ash, her sorrow drifts beneath the skies:
she knows not what is lost nor why she cries.

THE FALL OF ROME

When Odoacer finally shut down
the last of the imperial puppet shows,
it seems that almost no one in the town
noticed the empty stage, the drama's close.

For what old Romans would have thought disaster
awakened in the young no apprehension.
But slow surrender gave Rome a new master,
though Romulus Augustus got a pension.

ANONYMOUS CREEK

It runs brown with the tannins of the leaves
of white oak, walnut, hickory, and ash
that, like confetti, flock so gently down
and land so lightly that they make no splash
or ripple in the brook's face as it weaves
and wanders here along the edge of town.

Too dark and shallow for a fish's dream,
too insignificant to sport a name,
it dribbles over pouting lips of shale
and carves its signature in stone the same
as any pedigreed and deeper stream,
burrowing into earth to form the vale

that is its final legacy. We, too,
run quietly in autumn, waters stained
dark like tea by all that has been cast
into our course, defined as we're constrained,
and wear against the bedrock till we're through
cutting a coulee that we hope will last.

FRANCIS AFTER COLLESTRADA

Our army met Perugia's on the plain
beside the hospital. All day we fought
with crossbow, sword, and lancet to obtain
our freedom, but by dusk it came to naught.
Then I became a prisoner of men,
as glorious as a rat holed in its nest,
and mourned for joys I might not taste again,
considering him pierced the truly blessed.
But skulking home, I gained some intimation
of grace in watching lepers beg their food
and learned no earthly city is my nation
and that affliction borne can proffer good.
For Heaven holds neither Ghibelline nor Guelph,
but those whom God abases for himself.

THE WAY OF GEESE

October come, the Canadas take air
like hopeful seed cast into frost's despair.

Autumn makes claims. Geese do not try to hold
the line of summer against the coming cold,

but heroically surrender to each season
what must be given up. This is the reason

they mount the invisible stairs of heaven and fly
in an alphabet of grace against the sky.

Their glyphic flights are oracles for me:
gains bind us to this world, but losses free.

www.ingramcontent.com/pod-product-compliance
Lightning Source LLC
LaVergne TN
LVHW020650100826
845148LV00012B/2407